"*The Green Notebook* gives one the key to enter the extraordinary poetical world of John Angell Grant. It is a world constituted of the lyrical and the horrific, the serene and the troubled, the desired and the lost. It is a world forever in motion and the poet at its center is Whitmanian in his ceaseless engagement with everything coming his way. The encounters might result in a witty and off-the-cuff haiku or, just as likely, a sober and well-wrought sonnet. Versatility leads the way. The poems about his father are unforgettable in their anguish and the poems finding peace in the simplicity of the everyday are consoling. Above all, this collection gives us a poet fully present in a reality he has been given and which he redeems." –**William M. Chace, Professor of English and President Emeritus of Emory University, author of *The Political Identities of Ezra Pound and T.S. Eliot.***

"John Angell Grant has written a splendid collection of poems, compassionate and eloquent, comprising the daily, often represented by his cat, the awful, most represented by his father, and the inevitable, with sad incisive thoughts about Death. They help us confront our lives, both in their trivial and more profound aspects." – **Peter Stansky, Frances and Charles Field Professor of History, Emeritus, Stanford University, author of *The Socialist Patriot: George Orwell and War.***

"*The Green Notebook* offers rueful wry wit haunted by hideously violent childhood abuse. Now grown old, Grant savors solitude and compassion in a garden ringed by mirrors, crossing to the other side and back, entering realms of hurt and delight with direct clear spoken verse and quirky sonnets. An astonishing and moving book." – **Hilton Obenzinger, Associate Director Emeritus, Chinese Railroad Workers in North America Project at Stanford University,** author of the poetry collection *Witness: 2017-2020.*

"Okay, dahlink, I read the whole thing. I found it oddly comforting, especially "Moving Toward Death." I like the snarky sonnets especially. Also "Le Carnet Vert" (I lived in Paris for many years). I think your work would very much suit The New Yorker. You're strange, there's no doubt about it, but most of my favorite people are similarly afflicted. Thank you for entrusting me with your fine work. And I don't even like cats in general. I think they know too much. Plus one of the neighboring feral pussies kicked my little dog's ass." – **Raechel Donahue, kick-ass disc jockey at San Francisco's KSAN radio and Los Angeles' KROQ.**

# The Green Notebook

Poems on
Family, relationships, spirituality, self-enquiry, recovery, ACA,
disruption, death, walking through the mirror, and cats

By
John Angell Grant

Also by John Angell Grant:

Women and Religion in the Modern Drawing Room: Plays of
T.S. Eliot

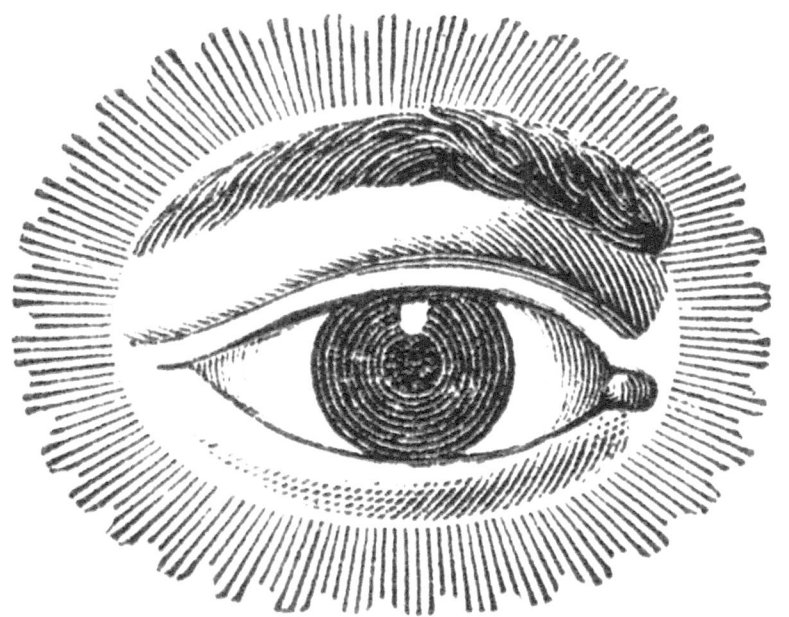

# PUBLISH

EYEPUBLISHEWE
PUBLISHING POETRY, LITERATURE, ART, MUSIC
FOR HUMANITY'S SAKE
A BRAND NEW PUBLISHING COMPANY
SAN FRANCISCO
FOUNDED 2020

For Martha Elizabeth Angell, thank you

# Contents

1: **Lift Off** ...................................................................... 1

The green notebook .......................................................3

At five years old ...........................................................5

A blind man dreams that he has recovered his sight 8

Sonnet: I think about the end ....................................9

Sonnet: Free verse is like anarchy ...........................10

The birch tree ...............................................................11

I asked my father once .................................................13

The bird mirror .............................................................14

So here's the thing .......................................................15

Family life ....................................................................16

Pat's passing .................................................................18

Haiku ............................................................................23

Ouch ............................................................................24

Sonnet: I can see the tunnel .......................................25

The Poetry Doorman ...................................................26

2: **Landing** ...............................................................29

The tribe......................................................................31

When I tell the story ...............................................33

3: **The other world** ..............................................39

Near-Death Experience [Vers. 3] .......................41

Foot reflexology.......................................................45

4: **Lateral movement** .........................................49

End of a romance.....................................................51

Sonnet: Another death song................................53

Arugula.......................................................................54

The cat walked across my head............................56

I slipped out of the primary.................................58

Self-enquiry...............................................................61

5: **Bottoming**........................................................65

Sonnet: To death .....................................................67

The critical inner parent departs .......................68

6: **Crawling**............................................................73

Sonnet: Can I push through death......................75

Walking through a mirror .....................................76

Writing a sonnet in the dark ...............................79

7: **Freedom** ............................................................81

Floating towards death ............................................. 83

Sonnet: We float towards death ............................. 85

Writing a sonnet ....................................................... 86

8: **Breakthrough** .................................................... 87

My father liked to pick the cat up ......................... 89

Pale Fire .................................................................... 92

The Other Side of the Wall..................................... 95

Tatters ....................................................................... 97

Cat Travel 2 .............................................................. 99

9: **Side steps** ........................................................ 103

If Prilosec causes dementia.................................. 105

Old friend ............................................................... 107

10: **Grace** ............................................................. 109

If I spit into a DNA tube ...................................... 111

In the playground .................................................. 116

Moving from the analog age................................ 117

Haiku: Honor......................................................... 119

Non-poem ............................................................. 120

The transformation point..................................... 123

Wordle.................................................................... 124

Sonnet: On deathwatch (Death 2) ............................125

Writing a sonnet .......................................126

The most beautiful women in the world ................127

Le carnet vert ........................................130

Christmas during the pandemic ............................133

24 hours .............................................136

Acknowledgments ......................................138

About the author .......................................139

About EYEPUBLISHEWE ....................................140

# 1: Lift Off

# The green notebook

As the cat steps slowly out
A side door
And into the backyard,
She sees a bright green notebook
Sitting on a garden table,
Under an umbrella,
Sheltered from the misty rain.

She jumps up on the table,
Finds a dry spot,
And sits next to the notebook;
Which she understands
Is a source of love.
She suspects I will sit at that table also,
And she wants to be with me.

The sun is low in the morning winter sky.
The rain now falls steadily.
This is good,
Because California is thirsty.

Joining the cat
Under the large garden umbrella,
I seat myself
In a dry chair,
And listen.

One bird calls,
Lonely,
In the distance.

Water splashes into the gutter
And lightly onto the ground.

The rain has something to say.
I don't speak "rain" fluently,
So I will translate the best I can.

It seems to say,
"Be kind to yourselves,"
As it wets the dry ground.

Then it continues,
"And be kind to others.
We are here for only a short time.
Enjoy your momentary spark of earthly existence.
Soon it will be gone.
Here is some water."

I look at the cat,
She looks up at me.

We understand today's message,
Which is now written
In the green notebook.

John Angell Grant

# At five years old

At five years old,
I came down the stairs
And saw my father
Sitting on top of my mother
Beating the shit out of her.
I was frightened.

He had been fucking
A nurse
On his overnights
At medical school,
And my mother
Apparently said
That she was going to leave him.

When Dad saw me
Enter the living room,
He leapt up
Off my mother
And shouted,
"You little shit!
I will thrash you
To within an inch
Of your life!"

I was frightened.
I ran upstairs
And locked myself
In the bathroom.

My father pounded
On the door.

"Open this door,
You little shit!"
He shouted.

I whimpered.

A few days later
My mother put herself
And two small children
On a plane
To California.

We stayed with her parents
In Walnut Creek.
I loved it.

John Angell Grant

Two months later
My father visited,
And apparently some
Reconciliation was reached.
It was the 1950s,
And my mother's family
Told her it was her duty
To support her husband.
So back we went to
Brookline, Massachusetts,
To the apartment
We inhabited
While my father
Was a student
At Harvard Medical School.

And once again,
It was bad.
And things got worse,
But that's a whole
Other story.

# A blind man dreams that he has recovered his sight

A blind man dreams that he has recovered his sight.
He can see the village square in front of him,
As he sips his blackberry tea
At a table
Outside a café.
The morning is sunny,
The weather fair,
The women beautiful.
His spirits soar.

Down the street a tortoiseshell cat
Chases a dead leaf.

Can it always be like this, he wonders.

The man pays his bill, rises
And walks to the river.
Two boys are skipping stones.
Soon he treks back to his cottage,
And sits down again,
This time in an armchair on his front porch.
He falls asleep; and when he wakens
He can no longer see.
He is blind again.

John Angell Grant

# Sonnet: I think about the end

I think about the end, and wonder what
That means. "The end." It drifts away
When I focus on it. (The mind can blunt
Itself when managing a narrow say.)
So I look again, now see an open
Door, through which extends a vista landscape,
Wider than my former concept, loping,
A free and endless, flowing sweet escape,
Undraped from worldly clutching hand; now fear
Gone, left behind, released to clouds of noth-
Ingness, dissolved and vanished; my heart clear,
Like a new-born, soon disappearing moth.
Death, I love you. Death you are my true friend,
Leading me to light, not to a darkening end.

# Sonnet: Free verse is like anarchy

Free verse is like anarchy, blank verse is
Like democracy; sonnets are old class
Society, vertical, structured, "his"
Moderated, enforced timely hourglass
Turning, playing by rules. Tho this sonnet
Is more a dress-up party. Come as Ed-
Ith Wharton's boyfriend or girlfriend, bonnet
In hand, hopping off your brougham, beach-head
Party in long-dress awaiting, spittoons
On the sand; just rhyme your lines and count your
Feet, two here, two there, hit the dessert spoon's
Second beat; or its first, if your clangor's
Being bold (trouble-maker, you), have fun,
It's all a game, the game of rhyme beat spun.

John Angell Grant

# The birch tree

I stroll slowly by a hole in a wall,
Surveying its curious opening.
The wall is red brick,
And the hole is
Two feet in diameter,
Where bricks
Are punched out.

When the hole
Moves around
Within the wall,
I am surprised.

I decide to pass through this opening.

I back up carefully,
Time my start,
Lunge towards the gap,
Dive,
And make it through to the other side.

My right shin is scuffed,
But no matter

Because there on the other side
The world is green.

I lie down in the grass,
In the shade,
Under a birch tree,
And dream.

John Angell Grant

# I asked my father once

I asked my father once,
Why he was unkind
To our family.

His response was,
"Take your sickness,
Shove it up your asshole,
And take it 2,000 miles away."

Then he went
Back to his job
As Director of Pathology Education
At the University of Texas
Medical Branch
At Galveston.

[Soon he was fired
From that job.]

# The bird mirror

A bird is trying to fly into
One of the garden mirrors.
He wants to visit his doppelganger.

He has been making this crossover attempt
For several days;
Arriving in the afternoon,
And spending three or four minutes
Flapping at the mirror,
Trying to get through.

Now sitting on a camelia branch,
Inches from the mirror,
He looks again at his new friend,
This time quietly,
And cocks his head.
He is enjoying this strange new acquaintance.
Yes, life is so interesting.
Without realizing it,
Our bird has wandered into the world
Of his own imagination.

John Angell Grant

# So here's the thing

So here's the thing:
I am not going to commit suicide.
I can guarantee you that.

The reason is,
There would be friends and relatives
Who would be devastated
If I did that.

Martha, for one.
My sister, for another.
My sister might not survive if I committed suicide.
That's a real possibility
So I won't do that.

I just wanted you to know,
In case you were worrying.

# Family life

My father monitored my mother's calls.
When I spoke with her,
I could hear the clicking of a telephone
On their bedroom extension,
And my father's breathing as he listened.

Dad told my mother
That if she flew from Dallas
To San Francisco
To visit her two children,
And her sister,
And brother-in-law,
That he would drive her
Up into the mountains,
And drop her off in a cabin,
Isolated,
With no phone
And no car,
And abandon her.
That is what she told me dad said.

When mom finally became
So debilitated
That she could not prepare
My father's meals,
Or do his laundry,
He called my sister in California,
And said about my mother,
"You take her;
She's no use to me now."

# Pat's passing

I'm drinking a coffee
At the Palo Alto Café
In Midtown,
Before nine in the morning,
During the pandemic.
The place has
A few
Scattered customers.
The street,
Out in front,
Is empty of morning rush hour traffic.
People are quarantined,
Working at home;
Or at home
Unemployed.

Two women at a table
Twenty feet away
Laugh
Over their coffee,
Having a great time;
Forecasting, perhaps,
A return to pre-pandemic normalcy.
Will that ever happen?

John Angell Grant

Now they are talking about
Voltaren versus CBD,
Two painkillers.
Oh, well;
It's the aging process;
Joints ache;
You have to find your own best therapy
For the stings of getting on.

This café is a place of memories
For me.
I came here often
During my early days in Palo Alto,
To sit, and read,
And write.

I need to thank Pat for that.
Pat, my partner for 15 years,
Who passed away
Thirteen months ago,

Hidden in her house in Pacific Grove,
Giving her French boyfriend
Of the moment
Strict orders
Not to tell anyone
Of her illness;
Or that she was dying.
Not one person.
Not even her brother.
It seems so sad.

But that was all very Pat.
I found out about her death
A few months later,
By accident, really
(That's the way Pat
Would have liked it;
Either to find out by accident
Or, better, not to find out at all).
But I heard it

John Angell Grant

From a former Barnard College
Roommate of hers;
A woman in shock,
As was I,
At the news;
Pat's French boyfriend,
Having sent a short obituary
To her college
Alumnae magazine,
Against Pat's explicit wishes, he later said.

Poor Pat.
The cancer got her.
As it gets many of us.
So it's amazing.
Sitting in this café,
Where I first sat 26 years ago,
During my first season in Palo Alto.
To have lived in a place for so long,
This is a new experience for me.
And so, too, now having the chance
To experience the nostalgia
Of sitting at a table
Where I sat often 26 years earlier.

I love Palo Alto,
This formerly quiet
Middle-class
University town;
Now turned, to its increasing loss,
Into a bubbling
Start-up incubator.
Where homes roll over
Again and again,
With seven figures
Added to the price
Each time.

Things have changed,
During my tenure here.
But this particular morning
At the café
Is wonderful.

So now,
With my coffee in me,
And some writing
Behind me,
It is time to move on,
Into the rest of this mysterious day.

John Angell Grant

# Haiku

Sometimes I get in-
terrupted in the middle
of a poem and

# Ouch

Part of being a poet
Is the responsibility I have
To drag my heart
Through the underbrush,
Over the rocks,
Onto the dirt path,
And into the lake.

It's a rough journey.
My heart gets scratched,
Pinched,
Torn open in places,
Poked with nettles,
And finally,
Dunked in the water.

The splash is a relief,
Though it stings.

So that's what it's like to write a poem.

And if I wrap my heart in "gauze,"
Before setting out,
The poem won't be as good.

John Angell Grant

# Sonnet: I can see the tunnel

I can see the tunnel that leads to my
Death. There it is, right in front of me, curv-
Ing into the exit's flow, where it spills, dies
And flies out the chute into a quick swerve,
(Splash!), now become nothingness, vanished from
The sky. Bright points of light, dots here and there,
Silent and twinkling, black surrounding them.
How? When? Why ask those questions, sweet nowhere,
As here we go, down the chute into joy,
A roller coaster ride, flying deathward,
Where happiness and release soon deploy
Our spirits, which fade into beauty unmarred
By scars of the material world's need--
And gone: fear. Finally released and finally shed.

# The Poetry Doorman

Sometimes a poem is like a door stop;
It holds open a door
Through which I can walk
To freedom.

Whew;
It's nice to be on the other side of things.
Where the grass is green,
And the birds are chatting away,
And the laissez-faire cat is sleeping in the sun,
Ignoring those birds.
Life is good.

Back through on the other side of the poetry door,
However,
Things look darker.
I peer into the shadowy opening,
From where I came.

John Angell Grant

Though it's dark
I can hear something;
A little rustling;
What is that?
I can't tell.
I strain.
Then,
In the distance,
I hear a train speeding up,
Blasting its horn.

It has been suggested that I not close this door.
That was the recommendation, at least,
From the poetry doorman.
Maybe doorman is the wrong word.
He was a happy guy
Sitting on a stone
Near by
When I first passed through.
I asked if I needed a ticket,
He shook his head, "No."
So I came through.
"Just don't close the door,"
Was all he said.

# 2: Landing

# The tribe

What is the nature
Of a tribe?
I don't have
A tribe.

My social limbs
Were hacked off
Early.

My father's social limbs
Were hacked off
Early.
He had none.

*His* father had 11 wives,
And abandoned
Them all.

To prepare
For leaving a wife,
Grandpa would take
Money from her purse,
Tiptoe out the back door,
Go down to the station,
Hop on a train,
Leave town,

And never look back.
He discarded many women
And many children,
And hurt many people.

His son,
My abandoned father,
Was nutso.

So what is a tribe?

I am one of those people
(And there are many of us)
Who lives alone,
Behind a closed door,
Peering out occasionally,
Venturing out from time to time;
But basically a solo act.

By choice
Detached.

Yes, there are many of us
Who, by preference,
Live isolated.

We have no tribe.

John Angell Grant

# When I tell the story

When I tell the story
Of my father crushing
My chest as a child,
I release sadness
Into the world.

I understand why people
Don't want to hear this ballad,
But it is my song,
And a sad air it is.

When I go back and
Read those suffocation poems myself,
I feel an assault of the pain.
So I understand why others
Wince
When I tell that story.

People, in fact, ask me to stop
Telling the story,
The story of my father
Crushing my chest
Until I couldn't breathe.

It is a painful story to hear,
And they don't want to hear it.
I understand that.

What has been surprising,
However,
Is to see how others
Project their own pain.

Family members and friends
Ask me not to share
My experience
Of having my chest and lungs
Crushed by my enraged father
When I was small,
Because, they say,
It is not good
For *me* to relate that story.

But I can't help it.
The pain is so severe,
I must cry out in agony,
And release it.

John Angell Grant

I understand that others suffer,
However,
When hearing the story,
And how they want to end
Their experience
Of suffering,
By silencing the singing of my song.

Sometimes they tell me that they are
Doing this
For me,
To help me to stop
Feeling my pain.

But that is not how it works.
They are asking me to silence
So that they do not
Feel the pain *themselves*.

They are practicing a transfer
Of their pain onto me,
As a mechanism,
They hope,
That will staunch their own
Feelings of pain
At hearing the story.
I understand how it works.
No one wants to
Feel that pain.

But I'm sorry,
I must sing this song.

John Angell Grant

And when I turn the pages
Of this notebook,
And hear this story being sung,
The pain is unbearable.

The Green Notebook

# 3: The other world

# Near-Death Experience [Vers. 3]

Darn,
Once again, I missed my poetry writing time.
Usually it's in the morning.
Today, instead, I had a zoom meeting with a friend
Who's confined.
She's older,
And in assisted living;
Where I'll be
In a few years,
If I don't first stumble,
Trip over my neuropathic feet,
Hit my head on the pavement,
And die.
Which is a possibility.

An acquaintance remarked
The other day,
That I was talking a lot
About death.
His comment surprised me.
Yes, I had mentioned death;
But just an ordinary amount;
Not a lot.
So I said that to him,
And he seemed to agree.

How can one not talk about death?
It's where we all go.

In my personal near-death experience,
Decades ago, in Athens,
I floated up to the ceiling,
And began the process of dying,
Moving slowly along the top of the room
Toward some kind of exit tunnel.

During this wafting journey,
I looked down at my travel friend,
Sitting at a desk
In our pension room below,
Writing a letter,
And realized I was dying.

I felt no fear
At that realization,
And no grief.
Rather, I felt some joy.
I was going through an unburdening;
Shuffling off the mortal coil;
It was a release.

John Angell Grant

And then my 106-degree fever
Which had been steadily climbing
(a reaction to that day's cholera shot),
Suddenly broke,
And I reversed my direction.

Now I floated back the other way,
Away from death,
Back towards where I had come from;
Out of the tunnel,
Now hovering momentarily just below the ceiling,
Then looking down at my body on the bed,
And descending slowly,
Towards that bed,
And back into that body,
Which was
Lying there quietly.

The experience was striking;
And it has stayed with me.
I learned that death
Contains release and joy.
It is the survivors who suffer.
It is they who experience
Loss and grief.

For the deceased, however,
Death can be joyous.

For me, at least,
That was my experience.

So why *not* discuss death?
It seems important.
Everyone knows about it.

And I'd like to repeat this,
My personal experience:
Death, per se, is not a bad thing.

It is the living
Who suffer.

John Angell Grant

# Foot reflexology

I told two friends
Last week
About my experience
With foot reflexology,
And they said,
"Well, even it it's
Only psychological,
And it's helping you,
That's good."

I was startled.
I said to one,
"For me, it's all science."

She tried not to laugh
In mockery.
Again, I was startled.
I've had powerful
Results from the practice,
And from my 50 years of practice
Of Taoist breathing and meditation,
Taught by
A Taiwanese tai chi master
In San Francisco
In 1972 and 1973.
Such practice,
A cousin to Chinese medicine
And to foot reflexology,
Showed me
The power of "chi" in healing.

In Chinese medicine
The words for
"breath" and "health" and "energy"
Are the same: chi.

John Angell Grant

So anyway, I was reminded
By my two friends'
Mockery of the practice
Of foot reflexology
That some people
Will understand
What I'm talking about,
And some people
Will not.

# 4: Lateral movement

# End of a romance

My girlfriend
Gave me a coffee mug
That she bought
In Mexico,
When she moved out
Of our apartment.

She had a
New boyfriend.

"Here," she said,
"I want you to have this."

I looked at the coffee mug.
I was so sad.

Later,
She told me
That she had stopped
Drinking from
That coffee mug
Because she feared
It was glazed
With lead,
And she didn't want to get
Lead poisoning.

I had to laugh.
I thought about her gift
For a few moments,
And then
Tossed it
In the trash.

John Angell Grant

# Sonnet: Another death song

Another death song. It just floated by.
There it is! A patchwork in the sky so
Close. Wow, look at that: radiant, large-eyed
Death, staring. And me, drifting cargo.
I open the patchwork flap. Inside there
Is more sky, like a Rene Magritte paint-
Ing. I crawl through the jumbled hole's nightmare,
Onto the other side. Wump. Unrestraint.
So here I am, at the other side of
Death. Hmm. Not so bad. Not so different.
Freer, actually. Joy. Light of love.
What a surprise. Who knew, itinerant?
So now both sides are open. I walk back
And forth, no longer sad amnesiac.

# Arugula

I threw an empty
Arugula bag
In the trash.

It still contained
One tiny leaf fragment,
The size of a penny.

I thought,
"I don't need that."
Moments later
I went back to
The trash bin,
Took out the bag
And removed
The arugula leaf.

It resisted.
It didn't want to come out.

I thought,
Wow, here I am
Wrestling an arugula bag
For a tiny piece of leaf,
The size of a penny.
Is this the right thing to do?

John Angell Grant

Yes, responded the Pacific Ocean,
My higher power,
This is the right thing
To do.

So I extracted the leaf fragment
And put it in my smoothie.

And now I am moving forward
With the rest of my day.

# The cat walked across my head

The cat walked
Across my head this morning,
And invited me
Out of my dream.

I resisted.

Life was
Simpler
In the dream;
The world was
More colorful;
There was
Urgency
And love,
In the dream,
That I wanted
To address.

But the cat understood this.

John Angell Grant

So she lay down
Next to me,
On her side,
Pushed her paws
Up against my chest,
And together we
Fell back
Into sleep.

# I slipped out of the primary

I slipped out of the primary
Level of reality,
Into a narrow
And unremarkable
Walkway,
That turned away from
The main street.

There I found myself
In a place
That didn't exist,
Later on.

Because when I went back
To look,
It wasn't there.

But in that present moment,
It was real.
I walked down a
Narrow passageway.

John Angell Grant

There I found a café,
My dream café,
Like the ones in Rhodes,
Or Puerto Vallarta,
Or Siracusa,
Or Ravello.

I purchased a pour-over
Mexican coffee.
Five bucks,
Plus a dollar tip.
It took seven minutes
To brew.

I don't drink coffee,
Not much these days,
So I was racing.

The seats and tables
Were outdoors,
Under canopies.

It was a sunny spring afternoon.
Some young people worked
On their laptops,
Others chatted.

I was elated.
I wrote five poems.

It was like earlier days,
Engaged at a source
Of my inspiration.

I thought,
I am so happy.

But the next day,
When I went back,
This back alley cafe
Had disappeared.

John Angell Grant

# Self-enquiry

I asked myself the question
"Who am I?"
And found that I didn't exist.

Instead, I discovered an awareness
Of my mind.
And when I held that awareness, it
Descended downwards,
Towards my heart,
Blossomed to a wider experience,
And then seemed to vanish.

A channel had opened.

But for me, that was the tricky part,
Holding open the channel
Of evolving nothingness from brain
To heart.

Because that's where my injury is,
The suffocation trauma
Of my father pressing his hand
On my infant chest,
In the first weeks of my life,
To stop my infant crying;
And causing me to black out.

I carry pain, fear and injury there,
In that part of my chest.
And while returning to the source of the injury
In a mindful way
Is healing,
It is also terrifying.
I find myself holding my breath;
I get scared;
I can't breathe.
These are sub-rational PTSD body reactions.
I strive to hold steady through them.
It is challenging.

Because when I bring attention
To the upper part of my chest,
Where the trauma lives,
My awareness of that injury
High-tails it,
And I run away also.

The irony, of course,
Is that the physical injury and trauma in my chest
Took place decades ago,
And the perp is now long deceased.

John Angell Grant

But when I go there,
With my mental attention,
In the process of meditating,
The body reacts.
It winces.

And when I return attention to the area,
One more time,
It winces again,
And impels me to flee again,
Though perhaps less so,
With a growing mindfulness
Of the history of the injury,
And the new kindness
I'm bringing to it.

I hope to get past this injury.
I'm working on it.
It's like a railroad spike
Nailed through my chest,
Though the spike is beginning to soften

# 5: Bottoming

# Sonnet: To death

Caught in a death spiral. Then, sudden, shot
Out, into a float. Opening, easy. Still
Dead, however. Composed. Clear mind. Blind spots
Cleared; fret dissolving; eyes open; war hill
Back-sliding. Set free we float through sky night
Stars, then day-blue skies, searching nowhere now
But here, seeing, listening, radiating light,
Or darkness, as it may be. Wow, sweet wow.
My pieces are gone, broken in the void,
Shattered, scattered to the breeze and heat and
Cold; run peacefully, unmerging, clash-joyed;
Till ne'er meets now and now meets land.
And land dies, flinging us back into dark
Lit sky, where we travel, or disembark.

# The critical inner parent departs

I'm crawling
Out of a cave,
In a daze.
The sun is out.
It is startlingly bright.
The hillside around me
Bright green.
The birds are chattering.

When I first inched forward,
There was silence.
As I held and listened,
I heard nothing.
Later, in the distance, one bird spoke,
Then another,
And a third.
Now they are in conversation.

The critical inner parent
Has been shown the door
By my world-class loving inner parent.

The earth is serene.
My shackles have dropped off.

John Angell Grant

I sit down on a rock.
A cat appears.

She runs over
And jumps up
Into my lap.
She is sweet.

I stroke the sides of her head,
She loves that.
Then I set her down,
Stand,
And walk to the edge of the garden.
Though still January,
And nippy,
I can feel spring announce its presence
In the far distance,
In this world of climate change.

The birds are talking about it.

I am fortunate.
My life is clear,
And my choices are open.

I understand that dark thunder
Can creep up on me
When my mind goes drifting,
Without care.
That is the critical inner parent
Trying to sneak back in.

But then,
My world class loving inner parent
Can step in
And kindly ask him
Please to leave.

It's like a Norse fairy tale,
Where the critical inner parent
Turns to smoke
And blows away.

For me, it's a process.

How to conduct my day?

It turns out I love listening to stories.
I got that early on.

John Angell Grant

My mother loved to read,
Though she was mostly silent
Around me,
Afraid to speak.

My father told stories,
About himself.
His whole life was
One string of stories.
Stories of his great success,

As he framed them,
And stories of early childhood
Deprivation and tragedy.

It's hard to know what the reality was,
His stories were so colored
By his act of story-telling.

So just tell stories.
That was a lot of the message I heard.

And thus, here I am,
Relaxing in the garden,
Having just exited the cave,
Sitting next to the cat,
Who has now hopped up
On her own chair,
Telling you a story.

The sun has risen further.
It is now warmer,
Especially for January.
Someone rattles a can in the distance,
And the birds go silent.
What a lovely day.

In one week,
I turn 75 years old.

John Angell Grant

# 6: Crawling

# Sonnet: Can I push through death

Can I push through death to life and find light?
Yes, it happens to me daily; go fig-
Ure. It seems unlikely at the midnight
Of demise, but then I open the brig
Door and step through, into the vast radi-
Ance of all, and light is streaming every-
Where. Death is gone. Or maybe it's here, shady
No more. Instead joyous, open, airy.
What if, what if, what if? Who can feel her
Thoughts and dreams, sinking downward from the mind
And through the heart, walking on air,
And into the wide-open space aligned
With quiet creatures in and out; and nois-
Y ones, as well, now freed, now god's happy tomboys.

# Walking through a mirror

I sit in the back garden.
Several large mirrors
Lean against
The red brick wall.
They create openings
Into the wall,
And enlarge the size of the garden.

It is warm for mid-November.
The air feels magical,
As glowing sunless sky
(No blue showing)
Drapes its broad cloud curtain
Overhead,
Filtering light from its other side
Into this grey brilliance.

Two garden fountains bubble songs.
It is mid-day.
The birds are gone.

Today I have been released
From my search for the meaning of life.
I can breathe.

John Angell Grant

I walk to one of the garden mirrors
And step through.

I am now in the reverse world.
Which is similar to the world
I have just exited,
But flipped.

I stroll through this alternate world.
My neighbor wears his wedding ring
On the right hand.
He waves.
We talk about the color of his lawn,
How green it is.

I look down at my feet.
The cat has followed me through the mirror.
She knows something has happened.
She stays close.

I like this alternate reality.
Could I move here,
Settle down?
I know the cat would join me.
We could take walks together;

And occasionally,
Like Alice,
When the impulse strikes,
Step back through the mirror,
And visit the old country.

John Angell Grant

# Writing a sonnet in the dark

I'm writing a sonnet in the dark. I
Can't see anything. My shirt is black. My
Gloved hands are black. There is no light, aerify
My brain, please. I need help. Demystify
The dark. Help. Please. How did Milton do it?
Writing poems with no eyes. It seems im-
Possible. But maybe things change; a tool kit
Opens, and off we go. It's just prelim.
Wait! No! See! I've forgotten to write a
B-line. Look, the first quatrain! It's a, a,
A, a. Then c, d, c, d. Siddhartha
Poached the alternating b-rhyme sluiceway
From the first quatrain's lines. Hooray. Hooray.
Not. I'm in the dark. I have no eyes. How
Did John Milton do it, pow, pow, pow?

# 7: Freedom

# Floating towards death

I float towards death.
There's no point in grabbling on
To a changing material world,
Hoping to make it eternal.

Rising in the morning
While it's still dark,
I sit in a garden
With two fountains bubbling.

Sky color changes from black, to gray.
Clouds form,
A faraway sun illumines their edges.
It is cold.
It is beautiful.
I wear my heavy winter coat,
Drink my hot cup of tea.

In the distance I hear a train.
I think of America
In its variant train eras:
Today shunting commuters to work;
In an earlier time moving agriculture,
Tools and supplies
Around the country.

Before that
A pre-European population

Shared resources.
At that time no one owned this territory,
Now fenced, parceled, defended.
It belonged to our shared spirit.

The morning comes to light.
Now trains run more frequently.
A crow slowly
Glides onto a tree branch
Overhead.

I drift farther from my dream state.
It evaporates
In the sunlight,
As I waft towards a simple illusion that I am
Scudding away from death,

While underneath
The transformation continues
And, like sand,
We evaporate in the wind.

John Angell Grant

# Sonnet: We float towards death[1]

We float towards death. No point to grab the world
Hoping to make it eternal. I rise
While it's still night, thin-peopled dreams unfurled,
And sit out in the garden, sans disguise.
The sky shifts from black, to grey, to blue. Slow-
Ly the garden fills with light. It is beau-
Tiful. In the distance a boxed train blows
Its commuter horn. How things change. Pre-coup
This land belonged to our spirit. Now par-
Celled and fenced, it's fought over. A large crow
Glides into the tree above. I move far
From my dreamworld, its once rich counterglow
Fading. But the transformation contin-
Ues. Like sand, we vanish in the wind.

[1] An alternate version of the previous poem.

# Writing a sonnet

Writing a sonnet is like shoehorning
An overwide foot into a smaller
Boot. Squeeze, push, squeeze. Darn. This hurts. Bring
The poetry aloe. I need to stir
My imagination, and find a bounce
That works up the ladder, or down the lad-
Der, of meter and rhyme, badder, madder,
Whatever. I'm still seeing nomad
Drift, wandering soul that I am, today
Here, tomorrow gone, with Death's splattering
Into space, gliding among the stars, may-
Be, maybe not, into superstring
Twang life, now here, now gone, soon not to breathe
A human beat, tho here a warp's enwreathed

John Angell Grant

# 8: Breakthrough

# My father liked to pick the cat up by her tail

My father was crazy,
With a mean streak.
He liked to pick up the cat
By her tail.
It was easier for hm
To grab her that way.
She didn't like him,
She scrambled and fought,
Scratched him,
And tried to run away.

"God dammit," my father would shout,
When scratched,
Blotting at the injury,
To demonstrate to us that
He had a medical degree.

Then he would realize
He needed to perform
For the family.

In response to which
He would scrunch his eyes
And stare off to the side,
And upward,
Offering his performance look

Of a being in intellectual analytical thought.
And then he would
Explain to us how
The cat had
Psychological problems.

And he would say,
"Hmm" a few times.
Like this:
"Hmm." "Hmm."
Like he was on the verge
Of a spectacular discovery.

He was the dumbest person
In our small family of four,
Because he lacked my mother's
Family genes, which the rest
Of us had.

John Angell Grant

But really,
It's just that he was a sociopath
And hurt the cat.
And didn't care,
And he didn't want us
To see what he had done.

And please,

Just remember
This is all a secret,
What I've shared with you.

# Pale Fire

The bird is back.
And this time he's
Brought a pal,
So there are two of them banging their beaks on the mirror,
Trying to fly through
To the other side.

It must be frustrating for them,
Hitting their heads on that reflecting glass,
Trying to break into another world.

I'm reminded of the opening poem in
Nabokov's novel "Pale Fire."
"I was the shadow of the waxwing slain
By the false azure of the windowpane."
I read that poem decades ago,
And those lines have stuck in my head:
The account of a bird flying into a window glass
That reflected the sky,
And knocking himself
Cold dead.

John Angell Grant

My bird guy,
However,
Who's been coming back all week,
Is a little different.
He sits on a branch
In front of the mirror,

Looking into the glass.
He then launches himself
At it
From a few inches away,
Flapping wings and knocking his beak
Against the mirror
As he tries to fly through it.
He is unsuccessful.
When the beak hits the mirror
There is an audible tap.
Sometimes there are two taps in succession,
As he tries again,
To fly through the mirror.

It's the same bird who comes every day.

Today, though, for the first time,
He brought a pal.
Maybe he thought
Two birds would have a better chance
Of passing through.

Usually, however, he is alone,
Trying, solo, to go through the glass frame
Into a new world of
Beauty and joy.

Isn't that where
Most of us
Want to go?

John Angell Grant

# The Other Side of the Wall

I lean into a door,
And pass through.

A voice from somewhere
Says,
"You're on the right path."

My next door, however,
Has vanished.

So I lean in again,
And there the door is.
I pass through again.

Now on the other side
Things are peaceful.

I hear the sound of water
Splashing in a fountain.
Nearby, a blue umbrella,
Planted in the ground,
Waves
In the wind.

The birds seem happy.
They have food.

On the ground

I see the shadows of their wings,
Flying overhead.

Mirrors placed against
A shaded red brick wall,
Reflect the sunlight.

This is a world of beauty.

John Angell Grant

# Tatters

Now at the gate;
Just standing,
Waiting;
Leaning towards the wall.

In my mind,
Restful.

Wondering, but without goals;

Happy.

Now I pass through the gate.

The movement is internal.
Its peace a gentle
Discarding
Of the colorful rags
Of the mind.

Those tatters unfurl and
Float,
Drifting first upwards,
Then, later, down over the wall.

Such beauty,
Revealing a new day.

John Angell Grant

# Cat Travel 2

The cat often likes to be
On the other side
Of the door.

When she desires this,
She mews,
And asks for
Doorman services.

"Let me go through,"
She says.

Obliging,
I rise,
And walk to the door.
I know what it's like to want to be
Somewhere else,
And I understand the joys
Of travel.

So when I open the door,
Slightly,
The cat steps slowly
Into its small gap,
And then unexpectedly stops,
Halfway through,
Taking time now
To consider her next move.

She requests that
My doorman services
Continue,
As she,
Momentarily suspended,
Considers her options.

I wait patiently.
I enjoy seeing
If I can out-wait the cat.
Often I can.
So we stand together,
Unmoving.

I wait patiently.
We have a good relationship,
The cat and I.

John Angell Grant

I love her,
And she loves me.
We bond
At this cautious beginning
Of her new adventure.

# 9: Side steps

# If Prilosec causes dementia

If Prilosec causes dementia
I guess I should stop taking it.

I've been consuming the medication nearly daily
For ten years.

A Harvard study now finds
That 44% of daily Prilosec users
Had an increased risk
Of dementia
Versus the non-medication takers,
In an eight-year study.

Again,
After eight years,
The non-medication takers had a 0% tendency
Towards dementia;
While the Prilosec takers had a 44% tendency
Towards dementia.

Those are serious data.

I've been feeling
More forgetful recently.
I've noticed it.
I'm going to stop
Taking the Prilosec.

# Old friend

My old friend from the 60s
Is still smoking weed daily,
Sitting in his garden,
And writing one-word poems,
Such as:
"Birds."

# 10: Grace

# If I spit into a DNA tube

If I spit into a DNA tube
Before I die,
Might I be reconstituted
At some point
In the future?

If the technology gets there,
And we don't first destroy the human race,
How would this
DNA reconstitution
Work?

Will they throw my chromosomes
Into some kind of genetic petri dish
And let me grow?

And then at some point,
After things cook
For a while,
Open the hatch
And out I walk into a garden?

Things might be crowded
By then,
With all kinds of dead people
Elbowing each other
To get back into life.

But let's assume we work
This part out,
And there's space for everyone,
With nice accommodations,
And good weather,
Plenty of food,
And we all come back.

Will there be family reunions?
All those generations?
Presumably.

At least for those of us
Who liked our families,
And want to be reunited
With them.

John Angell Grant

That sector will likely be
In the majority.
While the curmudgeons,
Who don't want
Anything to do
With their
Former families,
Will be in the minority.
I guess.
Actually, I'm not sure about that,

But I think so.
Anyway, what will all this mean?
Because I think it
May happen.
All this reconstitution
And coming back to life.

Will we be happy,
Being back with the parents and grandparents,
And great grandparents,
And great-great grandparents,
(Including the murderers in the family),
For as long back
As anyone remembered
To spit in a DNA tube,
Or leave bits of their

Moldy remains
In rotting coffins in the ground?

Let's take a best-case scenario:
Will it be like William Morris's novel "Utopia,"
Where folks work
An hour or two each day,
If they want to,
And spend the remaining free time
Working on their stained-glass projects,
Or their music,

Or various other art forms?
Will we get to travel a lot?
That would be nice.

Does everyone get to make movies
And tell stories?
At least those who so desire?
It's easy to make movies
These days,
On your smart phone.
I just took a class
On how to do that.

John Angell Grant

When our
Reconstituted DNA
Brings us back to life,
Will there be cooking classes?
How about gym time and Pilates
For those
Who so desire?

Gosh, it's starting to sound
Pretty good.
So if we do decide to reconvene
After our deaths,
I hope we can all give it
Our best try.
It might be pretty good.

# In the playground

There are no barriers
In the playground
For small children.

They run back and forth
Between reality and imagination.
"Reality" is the wrong word.
What's a better word?
Text me, if you find it.

Hurrying back and forth
Between realty and imagination,
The world is rich,
Filled with all possibilities.
One child stumbles in the sand
And laughs.
Another goes down the slide.

In the upcoming,
Managed-personality era
Of gene editing,
Will this childhood experience change?

John Angell Grant

# Moving from the analog age

Moving from the analog age
Into the digital age,
Has been quite an experience.

It's like being
Someone who grew up
With horse-drawn wagons,
And then suddenly took a ride
In an automobile.

It's not a mere technological jump,
More like a crack
In the landscape of reality:
Where the old reality
Gave you an undisturbed
Rolling scenic view,
That's now suddenly broken;
Like a fracture,
In the ground after
An earthquake,
With a chasm
In the middle of the street,
And one pedestrian curb
Shifted thirty feet farther north.

Space has been broken,
Like Picasso's cubist landscapes.

So let's celebrate this.
The experience is freeing;
And beautiful;
And a reminder
That we are
Filled with magic.

John Angell Grant

# Haiku: Honor

It's an honor to
Be loved, especially
By an animal.

# Non-poem

I just went and bought
A new tiny
Pocket notebook,
The kind I write poems in.

I'd earlier set out to walk
Without a notebook,
Because I wrote a good poem
Already
This morning,
And thought I was
Poem-depleted
For the day.
Then,
Suddenly,
In the middle of my walk,
I could feel a poem growing.

Poems are like plants,
Rooting downward into the earth,
And upward into the sky.
I could feel one pushing.

But now that I have
My quill
And parchment,
As it were,

John Angell Grant

The song plant has folded inward,
Bowed its head,
And gone silent.

That's not unusual;
Poems have their moods,
Like flowers,
And birds;
And humans.

No biggie.
In a new dawn,
Under rising sunlight,
It may emerge again.

But for the moment,
Like a cat,
It has curled up and gone to sleep.
Where the poem's hiding
Is anybody's guess.
It could be under the bed.
It could be in the
Neighbor's yard.
It could be in the attic.

It could even be hiding
In this new pen
That I just bought,
For the purpose of
Writing
In this new notebook.

John Angell Grant

# The transformation point

I'm exploring that transformation point
Where the mind sails
Into the heart
And vanishes.

It's a good place to spend time,
That transformation point.
I hope to spend more time there
In the future.

Wow. "Future."
That's one of those mind words.
Because, now in my heart,
On the other side of the transformation point
The future has
Vanished,
If you know what I mean.

# Wordle

Wordle,
Dordle,
Quordle,
Octordle,
Sedecordle,
Duotrigordle,
Sextaginta-Quattuordle

John Angell Grant

# Sonnet: On deathwatch (Death 2)

On deathwatch, scanning the horizon of
My demise--an end, or transition to
Holy nothingness, a scattered love.
I throw awareness across the sky. New
Unsheltered I feel dissolution creep-
Ing toward me, my feet dying, my skin drying,
Turning to parched leaves and desert sand. Sleep-
Y, now more sensors fade, spirit skying.
I feel good, now that I'm dead, relaxed. No
Stress here, fear gone, joy radiating light.
Simply being, breath releasing its plough,
Till all I see is love at time-stopped midnight,
While in the starry sky, the drifting void,
My light's reversed, displaced, and redeployed.

# Writing a sonnet

Writing a sonnet is like trying to
Squeeze the air back into a football. It's
Tricky. Plus, there's no pump. Just push, push, do
The work. Squeeze, squeeze, squeeze, until a few bits
Fall into place, and you get the contour
Just right, with hopefully no lumps on the
Side; or scratchy spots where it looks like your
Car ran off the road (oh, rats) and hit a
Guard rail, smashing in its side and losing
Some paint. See! A mixed metaphor! That's what
I'm talking about. A football oozing
Air, followed by an auto wreck. Jump cut:
This one's been hard. Unwinding a sonnet
Is tough; but I like it--so I'm on it.

John Angell Grant

# The most beautiful women in the world

Beautiful afternoon
Beautiful conversation,
Surrounded by folks in the café
Enjoying a coffee or tea or water
At tables
Chatting happily with each other
In the sunny
Palo Alto summer afternoon;
After two years in pandemic quarantine
Hidden away in their houses.

Mixed-race pairs and trios
Enjoying their lives.

So beautiful.
It's the world of the future.

(If we make it there.)

One Mediterranean fable says:
The most beautiful women
In the world
Come from Marseilles.

And why would they say that?
Because Marseilles was
A central
Mediterranean port
In the ancient world
Where it mixed races.

People arrived from Africa,
The Middle East,
Asia, via the Silk Road.

They met and
They mixed.
And soon arrived
The world's most
Beautiful women.

Anyway, I digress.

Sort of,
But not really.
It's just the coffee shop,
It's so mixed race here.

John Angell Grant

It makes me happy.
So now I come here every day,
To enjoy a glimpse
Not only into the present,
But into the future.

Are you ready for the
Most beautiful women
In the world?

# Le carnet vert[2]

Alors que le chat sort lentement
Par une porte latérale
Dans le jardin,
Elle aperçoit un cahier vert vif
Sur une table de jardin,
Sous un parasol,
A l'abri du crachin.

Elle saute sur la table,
Trouve un endroit sec,
Et s'assoit à côté du cahier;
Dont elle comprend
Que c'est une source d'amour.
Elle soupçonne que je vais m'asseoir là aussi,
Et veut être avec moi.

Le soleil est bas dans le ciel de matin d'hiver.
La pluie maintenant tombe régulièrement.
C'est bien,
Parce que la Californie est aride.

Rejoignant le chat
Sous le grand parasol du jardin,
Je m'assois

John Angell Grant

Sur une chaise sèche,
Et j'écoute.

Un oiseau appelle,
Seul,
Au loin.

L'eau éclabousse dans la gouttière
Et à peine sur le sol.

La pluie a quelque chose à dire.
Je ne parle pas « pluie » couramment,
Je vais donc traduire du mieux que je peux.

Elle semble dire,
« Soyez bons avec vous-mêmes »,
Tandis qu'elle humecte le sol sec.

Puis elle continue,
« Et soyez bons avec les autres.
Nous ne sommes ici que pour peu de temps.
Profitez de votre brève étincelle d'existence terrestre.
Ce sera bientôt fini.
Voici de l'eau. »

Je regarde le chat,
Elle me regarde.

Nous comprenons le message d'aujourd'hui,
Qui maintenant est écrit
Dans le cahier vert.

---

*trans. Marilyne Bertoncini*
2 This is a translation into French by Marilyne Bertoncini of "The Green Notebook," the first poem in this book. It was published in Jeudi des Mots

# Christmas during the pandemic

Christmas is empty this year.
The recordings of happy Santa songs
Are playing on the mall sound system,
But the mall is empty.
A straggler here and there,
Wandering aimlessly past windows,
Stopping for a moment
To look at a jacket,
Or a vase,
And then drifting on.

It's the year of the pandemic.
Actually, year two of the pandemic.
Jobs lost,
Supply chains broken,
People scattering to other geographies.

Is the human experiment concluding?
Have we had our chance and muffed it?
Scientists say that if the human race expires
Planet earth will recover
In full and rich radiance.
The birds will be happy,
The land-based wildlife will be happy.
The sea life will be happy.

The billionaire sci-fi boys
In outer space
Are doing what?
Waving their cocks at each other?
Mine's bigger than yours, bro!

That doesn't seem helpful,
Extending human conflict,
Acquisitiveness,
And treachery
Into space.
That looks dark.

The human race has tossed a turd
Into the ecological punch bowl,
And now we're paying the price.
Mother Earth is showing us to the exit,
With a little slap on the bottom
On our way out the door.

John Angell Grant

Back at the mall,
A young Chinese woman calls, "Dad, dad."
And catches up with an elderly bald man
With a white beard
And a cane,
And, it seems, perhaps,
Dementia,
As he gets up from his seat

And wanders off in the wrong direction.
He's lucky to have her,
A loving daughter.
She is lucky to have him,
Sweet old dad.

# 24 hours

It's Friday late afternoon.
I'm sitting in the garden.
The cat has joined me.
She followed me out of the house.
It's warm.
It was a day of walking,
Followed by tech.
A nice day.
Martha received a new iPhone
And the installer came by to take her
Through the set-up.

The garden birds are chirping.
We refilled the backyard feeders this afternoon.
Dang, our bird friends eat a lot.
We refill those feeders every 2 or 3 days.
"Martha's Café" I call it.

Two doves sit in the black birch tree,
One half-way up,
And the other at the top.
The two small garden fountains are bubbling.

Now it's Friday night.
We are in pandemic quarantine,
So there will be no visitors this evening.

John Angell Grant

We watched Minari last night,
A moving film about a Korean family
Farming in Arkansas.
I guess I should feel lucky.
I do feel lucky.
And grateful.
But also I feel sad.
I love you all.

I hope the human race can move forward
In a happy and healthy way.
I hope the animals
And other living things
Thrive with us.
I'll see you on the other side
Of it all.
Perhaps.

Yes, in some way,
I believe I will
See you all
On the other side of it.

# Acknowledgments

Thank you, Martha, for your supportive literary, artistic, and musical spirit, that helped make these poems happen.

And thank you, also, to the following people:

- Dane, for publishing this book, and for being a friend for so many years. Many of these poems were first read at "Time to Arrive," the weekly poetry open mic hosted online by Dane Ince.
- Tish, for your inspirational ideas.
- Marilyne Bertoncini, for your translation of "The Green Notebook" into "Le Carnet Vert," and for publishing both in Jeudi des Mots; and later (with editor Carole Mesrobian) in Mots de PaiX et d'Espérance.
- Candy Carter, Teri Hessel and Michael Breger, the editors of Tangents, who first published "We Move towards Death," "Free verse is like anarchy," and "I can see the tunnel."
- Suda Miller, who first published "Bird Mirror" in Behind a Door.

# About the author

John Angell Grant is a writer/director from Palo Alto, California. His short fiction films "Two Stoners" and "1958" won many awards. He is the author of 12 fully-produced stage plays; two serialized newspaper novels; a scholarly study of T.S. Eliot's late drawing-room comedies; dozens of short films; and hundreds of poems and pieces of journalism. He has degrees from Columbia and Stanford. For more information about Grant's writing, please visit www.JohnAngellGrant.com

# About EYEPUBLISHEWE

Eye publish ewe is a brand new publishing company, founded in San Francisco. Art, music, video, poetry, and other literature will find inclusive shelter here. Quality work produced by the artists' hearts, minds, and souls rather than commercial interests will have this as a home. All are welcomed with open minds and hearts and eyes to the future. Together we will publish art for humanity's sake.

## EPE titles

**Where Grasses Bend**: Poems from Portland to Steens Mountain in the Time of Plagues by **Mimi German** ISBN: 979-8-9870259-5-6

**The Whole Existential Novel**: The Journey from the Dark Side of the Rainbow to Satchidananda by **Dane Ince** ISBN: 979-8-9870259-0-1

**Good Grief...Please!:** A Dialogue with Death and Life by **Tish Ince** ISBN: 979-8-9870259-2-5

## EPE titles
## coming soon

**A House without Walls:** Existential Journeys and Love Poems to Mexico by **Lesley Constable**

**"Naturalzela del Amor"** poems in Spanish and English by **Martin Del Toro Gutierrez**

www.ingramcontent.com/pod-product-compliance
Lightning Source LLC
Chambersburg PA
CBHW020357130626

46549CB00006B/2310